Integrity
in the
College
Curriculum:

A Report
to the
Academic
Community

**The Findings and
Recommendations
of the Project
on Redefining
the Meaning
and Purpose
of Baccalaureate
Degrees**

D1293434

*Association of American Colleges
February, 1985*

The work of the Project on Redefining the Meaning and Purpose of Baccalaureate Degrees was principally supported by a grant from the Pew Memorial Trust. Additional funding was provided by the Ford Foundation, the Exxon Education Foundation, the Johnson Foundation and the Buhl Foundation.

Published by the
Association of American Colleges
1818 R Street, N.W.
Washington, DC 20009

Copyright, 1985

ISBN 0-911696-18-0

C ontents

oreword

Baccalaureate education has been and will continue to be a matter of prime importance to American life. Building on the foundations laid in elementary and secondary schools, it rounds off the education of students, enlarges their understanding of reality, and enhances their powers of intellect and judgment. It strengthens the capacities of individuals to grow as literate, educated persons and prepares them to pursue beginning careers in several professions as well as advanced studies as further preparation for practice in others. Above all, baccalaureate education makes a vital contribution to the health of American democracy. Leaders in a complex, pluralistic society require not only technical or professional expertise but the ability to make consequential judgments on issues involving the contextual understanding and assessment of multi-faceted problems.

Baccalaureate education is still the primary responsibility and distinguishing feature of American higher education. Well over half of the students enrolled in accredited two-year community and four-year colleges are taking courses creditable towards bachelors' degrees, and, more significantly, seventy percent of all degrees awarded by four-year colleges and universities are baccalaureates.

Mindful of these fundamental truths about baccalaureate education, the Association of American Colleges took stock of mounting evidence that undergraduate programs in American colleges and universities were afflicted by serious weaknesses. During the years 1979 through 1981, for example, three national commissions had issued reports calling attention to deficiencies in basic areas of undergraduate study; namely, in the humanities, in foreign languages and international studies, and in science education for non-science majors. These reports intensified a concern for the general condition of undergraduate education itself, a concern which had been spreading both on and off campuses throughout the seventies. It was apparent that the persistence of such weaknesses would soon undermine public confidence in higher education and also adversely affect advanced studies in graduate and professional schools. Because of its fundamental mission to address such basic issues of educational policy, the Association of American Colleges, in January 1982, began the Project on Redefining the Meaning and Purpose of Baccalaureate Degrees and established the Select Committee to oversee and guide its work. The Select Committee, which was instructed to report its findings and recommendations in three years was directed: to make a thorough study of the state of baccalaureate education, to promote widespread discussions among faculties and academic administrators about issues of basic educational policy concerning the primary mission of colleges and universities, and to formulate recommendations for improving programs leading to bachelors' degrees in all institutions of higher education. The underlying premise of this task was that piecemeal reform of undergraduate education had failed to check the deterioration in its condition, and hence a more fundamental, comprehensive approach to the problem was needed.

In surveying the growing body of literature about undergraduate education, the Select Committee concluded that more time and effort had been spent in analyzing the weaknesses of American college education than in determining effective ways to overcome them. It therefore invited the faculties and administrations of eleven colleges and universities to join in a year of discussion and inquiry to discover what measures for reform might be most appropriate for their institutions. To promote dialogue on these campuses, the Committee prepared a booklet, "A Search for Quality and Coherence in Baccalaureate Education," which suggested six lines of investigation. The year opened in the summer of 1982 with a conference at which a team from each of the eleven institutions were present, and closed with a week of intensive work at which the results of the year's discussions on each campus were summarized and shared with the Committee. Five different types of institutions were represented among the eleven:

1) *research and doctorate-granting universities:* Carnegie-Mellon University, University of Tennessee, Knoxville, and Washington University in St. Louis.

2) *comprehensive institutions:* Brooklyn College of the City University of New York, Rhode Island College, and Tuskegee Institute.

3) *liberal arts colleges:* Grinnell College, Hampshire College, and St. Mary's College of Indiana.

4) *community colleges:* Maricopa County Community College District.

5) *colleges for non-traditional students:* Empire State College of the State University of New York.

As a consequence of the issues raised but not settled by that year's work, two additional conferences were called to examine special concerns about professional baccalaureate degree programs in such fields as business, engineering, education, health sciences, and music. The first conference, attended by representatives from three campuses of the cooperating institutions that offered such degrees, took place at Gatlinburg, Tennessee, in October, 1983. The second, which involved elected and staff officers of all specialized accrediting bodies that evaluate baccalaureate programs, as well as liberal arts faculty and deans, was held at Airlie House near Washington in December, 1983. The results of these conferences confirmed one of the findings of the eleven cooperating colleges and universities, namely that "the very distinction between the 'liberal' and the 'vocational' that runs through two millenia of educational theory is no longer a universal." They further concluded that graduates with professional baccalaureate degrees as well as graduates with degrees in traditional liberal arts fields should share essential intellectual characteristics and attributes.

Other contributions to the deliberations of the Select Committee came from a special task group on assessment and evaluation of student progress and academic programs, and from a conference at the Wingspread Conference Center to consider how to reconcile recommendations on instruction in the humanities, foreign language and international studies, science instruction for non-science majors, and women's studies — recommendations which resulted from earlier AAC conferences at the same center. The last three Annual Meetings of the Association of American Colleges also developed information and insights of use to the Committee. The 1982 Annual Meeting on the theme "Literacy for the Contemporary World," the 1983 Annual Meeting on the theme "Liberal Learning with a Civic Purpose," and the 1984 Annual Meeting on the theme "A Tense Alliance: Specialization and Liberal Learning," all had principal speakers and working sessions which addressed issues under study by the Select Committee.

Throughout its deliberations, the Select Committee has taken all programs of baccalaureate education and all kinds of baccalaureate degrees to be within its sphere of concern. As a consequence, it has sought to encourage integrity and coherence in all undergraduate programs that lead to bachelors' degrees. This report is intended, therefore, for two-year community colleges responsible for providing foundations for students wishing to transfer to baccalaureate programs, as well as for four-year colleges. Its recommendations apply to undergraduate education in professional schools of business, engineering, allied health sciences, education, art, music, physical therapy, and nursing, as well as to the programs of liberal arts colleges and colleges of arts and sciences within multi-purpose campuses.

As it issues this report, the Select Committee is aware that some campuses have resisted the debilitating trends of the last generation. It also knows that many campuses of all sizes and types have already committed themselves to serious efforts to remedy the ills that have weakened undergraduate education. The Committee applauds this commitment and leadership, and hopes that the findings and recommendations of this report will sustain and accelerate the good work so promisingly begun. To the faculty, academic officers, and trustees of all campuses, the Committee offers this report as its best effort to assist them in developing undergraduate programs that match the needs and aspirations of their students.

Mark H. Curtis
President
Association of American Colleges

*A*cknowledgements

The work of the Project on Redefining the Meaning and Purpose of Bacca-laureate Degrees was guided by a Select Committee composed of the following American educators:

Arnold B. Arons, Professor of Physics, Emeritus, University of Washington

Ernest L. Boyer, President, Carnegie Foundation for the Advancement of Teaching

David W. Breneman, President, Kalamazoo College

Carleton B. Chapman, Professor and Chairman, Department of the History of Medicine , Albert Einstein College of Medicine, Yeshiva University

Martha E. Church, President, Hood College

Elizabeth Coleman, Professor of Literature and Humanities, New School for Social Research

Harold L. Enarson, Senior Advisor, Western Interstate Commission for Higher Education

Paul R. Gross, President and Director, Marine Biological Laboratory

Richard Kuhns, Professor of Philosophy, Columbia University

Arthur Levine, President, Bradford College

Theodore D. Lockwood, Director, Armand Hammer United World College of the American West

Robert H. McCabe, President, Miami-Dade Community College

Charles Muscatine, Professor of English, University of California/Berkeley

Leonard Reiser, Fairchild Professor, Sherman Fairchild Center for the Physical Sciences, Dartmouth College

Gresham Riley, President, Colorado College

Frederick Rudolph, Professor of History, Emeritus, Williams College

Linda B. Salamon, Dean, College of Arts and Sciences, Washington University

Jonathan Z. Smith, Robert O. Anderson Distinguished Service Professor, University of Chicago

Mark H. Curtis, *Select Committee Chair,* President, Association of
American Colleges

Benjamin H. Alexander served on the Select Committee while president of
Chicago State University and president of the University of the District of
Columbia. He resigned in March, 1984 upon joining the U.S. Department of
Education.

The report presented herein reflects the collective judgment of the members
of the Committee. Individual members of the Committee contributed to the
report at various stages. Harold Enarson, Charles Muscatine and Frederick
Rudolph served as an editorial committee and skillfully led the deliberations
which culminated in the first draft. Special thanks are due Frederick Rudolph
who put the findings and conclusions of the Committee into this final form.

The Select Committee gratefully acknowledges the indispensable assistance
that it received from the staff of the Association of American Colleges. William
R. O'Connell, Jr., vice president of the Association, aided by Diane Haddick,
program associate, and Elspeth Nunn, executive assistant to the president,
provided general coordination and administrative support for the Project.
Jerry Gaff, now dean of the College of Liberal Arts at Hamline University,
was the capable coordinator of the eleven institutions' work on the Project.
Edgar C. Reckard, Jr., formerly president of Centre College in Kentucky,
served as Senior Consultant during 1983-84, and chaired a special task group
to prepare materials on assessment and evaluation for the Committee. Diane
Haddick and Tom Haller provided research assistance and were responsible
for preparing bibliographies and collating background materials for meetings
of the Select Committee.

The faculty and academic officers of the eleven institutions that cooperated
with the Select Committee by conducting on-campus investigations of key
issues are too numerous to mention individually, but all contributed substantially to the Project. Among them, however, special thanks are due to several
persons: to President Robert Hess of Brooklyn College, CUNY, and Professor
Michael Gross of Hampshire College, who with Dean Linda Salamon of
Washington University, authored the final report on the institutional findings;
to Ralph Norman and Lee Humphreys of the University of Tennessee, Knoxville, who convened a special follow-up conference on undergraduate professional education; and to Anthony Penna of Carnegie-Mellon University,
John Jacobson of SUNY Empire State College and Willard F. Enteman of
Rhode Island College, who served conscientiously on a special committee to
prepare a principal supplement to the report. Finally, Jonathan R. Warren,
formerly of the Educational Testing Service, Dean Whitla of Harvard University and Robert Pace of the University of California at Los Angeles com-
prised an advisory committee on assessment and evaluation.

*T*he Decline and Devaluation of the Undergraduate Degree

The educational failures of the United States are emerging as a major concern of the 1980s. The abundance of reports diagnosing and prescribing for our schools and colleges, the urgency with which they are argued, the evidence that they summon, and the analyses that they offer are persuasive evidence that there is a profound crisis. Even though at first blush it may appear to be an exaggeration to say so, the recent critiques and analyses of American education are as vital to clarifying our condition as were the pamphlets of Tom Paine before the American Revolution and the speeches of Abraham Lincoln on the eve of the Civil War. When our committee was formed in 1982 we feared that our eventual report would be a voice crying in the wilderness. We now know that we have joined a chorus.*

Our report addresses the crisis in American education as it is revealed in the decay in the college course of study and in the role of college faculties in creating and nurturing that decay. Although effective remedies will require the dedication and energies and talents of many cooperating individuals and institutions, our own experience as teachers and as students of American higher education leads

*See Appendix for annotated list of reports.

to one inescapable conclusion: the college professors of the United States, whether they know it or not, have a job on their hands. They will need a great deal of help if they are to perform that job well. But, first, they and the American people must understand the nature of the problem and their shared responsibilities for meeting it. Because the decline of the undergraduate degree is at the heart of the problem, we must come to terms with that reality and develop some understanding of how we arrived where we are.

Evidence of decline and devaluation is everywhere. The business community complains of difficulty in recruiting literate college graduates. Remedial programs, designed to compensate for lack of skill in using the English language, abound in the colleges and in the corporate world. Writing as an undergraduate experience, as an exploration of both communication and style, is widely neglected. College grades have gone up and up, even as Scholastic Aptitude Tests and American College Testing scores have gone down and the pressures on teachers to ease their students' paths to graduate schools have increased. The modest gains in SAT scores in the June 1984 tests suggest a leveling off, but hidden in the statistics

1

are brutal social and economic facts: scores up dramatically in affluent Connecticut, flat in troubled New Jersey, down in New York City. Foreign language incompetence is now not only a national embarrassment, but in a rapidly changing world it threatens to be an enfeebling disadvantage in the conduct of business and diplomacy. Scientific and technological developments have so outpaced the understanding of science provided by most college programs that we have become a people unable to comprehend the technology that we invent and unable to bring under control our capacity to violate the natural world.

As for what passes as a college curriculum, almost anything goes. We have reached a point at which we are more confident about the length of a college education than its content and purpose. The undergraduate major — the subject, academic discipline, or vocational speciality in which a student concentrates — everywhere dominates, but the nature and degree of that concentration varies widely and irrationally from college to college. Indeed, the major in most colleges is little more than a gathering of courses taken in one department, lacking structure and depth, as is often the case in the humanities and social sciences, or emphasizing content to the neglect of the essential style of inquiry on which the content is based, as is too frequently true in the natural and physical sciences. The absence of a rationale for the major becomes transparent in college catalogues where the essential message embedded in all the fancy prose is: pick eight of the following. And "the following" might literally be over a hundred courses, all served up as equals. The chairman of the Committee on Economic Education for the American Economic Association, in a letter to AAC, recently admitted that "we know preciously little about what the economics major is or does for students" and then remarked that it is unlikely, whatever the major or institution, that the average graduating senior "has any integrated sense of his major discipline and its links to other fields of inquiry."

There is so much confusion as to the mission of the American college and university that it is no longer possible to be sure why a student should take a particular program of courses. Is the curriculum an invitation to philosophic and intellectual growth or a quick exposure to the skills of a particular vocation? Or is it both? Certainty on such matters disappeared under the impact of new knowledge and electives in the late nineteenth century. The subsequent collapse of structure and control in the course of study has invited the intrusion of programs of ephemeral knowledge developed without concern for the criteria of self-discovery, critical thinking, and exploration of values that were for so long central to the baccalaureate years. The curriculum has given way to a marketplace philosophy: it is a supermarket where students are shoppers and professors are merchants of learning. Fads and fashions, the demands of popularity and success, enter where wisdom and experience should prevail. Does it make sense for a college to offer a thousand courses to a student who will only take 36?

The marketplace philosophy refuses to establish common expectations and norms. Another victim of this posture of irresponsibility is the general education of the American college undergraduate, the institutional course requirements outside the major. They lack a rationale and cohesion or, even worse, are almost lacking altogether. Electives are being used to fatten majors and diminish breadth. It is as if no one cared, so long as the store stays open.

One consequence of the abandonment of structure by the colleges has been the abandonment of structure in the schools. The decline in requirements is contagious, and in the absence of system in national educational arrangements, articulation between secondary and higher education has been allowed to break down. The result is a loss of rigor both in the secondary and in the collegiate course of study. That loss of definition and rigor has encouraged the false notion that there is such a thing as effortless learning, a notion that finds expression in curricular practice and student behavior. As the colleges have lost a firm grasp on their goals and mission, so have the secondary schools.

Another consequence of the accelerating decline of the undergraduate degree is widespread contemporary skepticism about the quality of higher education. There is a public sense that standards are too low, that results are not what they used to be. Why have our colleges and universities turned loose on the elementary and secondary schools thousands of graduates unqualified to teach? Why have regional and specialized accrediting agencies been unsuccessful in arresting the debasement of baccalaureate education? Why have colleges and universities failed to develop systems for evaluating the effectiveness of courses and programs? Why are they so reluctant to employ rigorous examining procedures as their students progress toward their degrees? These are some of the questions that an uneasy public now addresses to those who bear the responsibility for the conduct of American higher education. The questions themselves are further evidence of the decline and devaluation that inspire them.

Why have the bachelor's program and the bachelor's degree fallen on evil times? Some of the difficulties are of historical origin, chronic illnesses that explain where we are but that defy easy remedies: the past cannot be repealed. Others are of more immediate origin, acute manifestations of the ways in which colleges and universities go about their affairs, set their priorities, and respond to the world around them. Some of these problems are caused externally and aggravated by insufficient and unimaginative internal response by the institutions themselves. Some of them are endemic today because of inconsistent and capricious policies of state and federal governments and the gradual abandonment by the faculty of its responsibility for the total curriculum.

For the first two hundred years of American higher education the course of study was shaped by the authority of tradition, seldom challenged and easily accommodating both new learning and changing social conditions. The degree — there was only one, the B.A. — was a passport to the learned professions; most of the nation's work was happily and effectively

3

done by people who had not gone to college. The American college at first was essentially a determined provincial echo of an English college.

The authority of tradition was undermined in the nineteenth century, particularly after the Civil War, by the emerging professional academicians. Holders of the Ph.D. degree, they were trained to be responsible to a particular body of knowledge, a discipline (English, history, biology) and to a style of learning that, although particular to that discipline, was shaped by the methods of investigation, concepts, and empirical values of science. The impact of their growing authority on the traditional course of study was immense: not only did many new disciplines and subjects find their way into the course of study but the concept of a wholly elective curriculum was advanced as an instrument for facilitating study of the new subjects. Faculty control over the curriculum became lodged in departments that developed into adept protectors and advocates of their own interests, at the expense of institutional responsibility and curricular coherence.

At the same time a dynamic and increasingly industrial society created new demands for technical skills, demands that were translated into formal bodies of knowledge that emerged in hundreds of new degree programs that challenged the supremacy of the B.A. degree, whatever its changing content. The emergence of the American university in the late nineteenth century—the result of the coming together of the English college tradition, the research ideal of the German university, and the American ideal of the university as an in-strument of public service—bombarded the old curriculum with an explosion of new subjects, courses, programs, and degrees. The American university developed into a magnificent democratic institution. Its libraries, laboratories, and scholars' studies became busy centers of inquiry, producing significant new knowledge at an accelerating rate. But dismay with the incoherence and lack of cohesion that resulted led in the early decades of this century to various devices to stem the tide of disarray: concentration and distribution, general education requirements, comprehensive examinations. By the time of World War II, tradition, the professional academicians, and society itself shared authority over what was going on in our colleges and universities.

Since World War II, American higher education has experienced a prolonged surge of growth. Colleges and universities more than doubled in number and many, especially public institutions, grew prodigiously. Enrollments in degree credit courses more than quadrupled. Bachelor's degrees more than trebled. The accelerating democratization of higher education—the opening of access, the tremendous numbers—has created in students a new and commanding authority over the course of study. The interests of students demonstrated by their selection of courses have increasingly helped to shape what has been taught, why, and how. What is now going on is almost anything, and it goes on in the name of the bachelor's degree.

The consequence of the dispersal of authority over the curriculum is the unhappy disarray, the loss of integrity in the bachelor's degree, that has called our committee into existence. We hold no brief for the curriculum of two centuries ago, but we do respect its coherence and its integrity. While acknowledging increasing attention in colleges to the review and upgrading of the general education component of higher education, we cannot ignore the grip of departmental autonomy and a misguided marketplace philosophy on the curriculum. Our mission is to assess the damage done to the bachelor's degree by the often conflicting and shared authorities that have supplanted tradition and to recommend ways in which the degree can be revitalized.

Another historical condition that defines the nature of American higher education is the vastness of the enterprise, its great diversity — old private universities, small liberal arts colleges, huge multi-campus state universities, community colleges, one-time teachers' colleges become state colleges, secular institutions and denominational institutions — over three thousand of them, every one a center of action and responsibility, every one in its own way defining the American experience in higher education. While this versatility and diversity is one of the great strengths of American higher education, it also accounts for the absence of common standards and expectations. Our federal system of government which distributes authority among fifty states and a central government in Washington also has contributed to the failure of the United States to develop a tradition of effective and respected national standards and expectations in higher education.

Until the development of the land-grant state colleges of agriculture and engineering after the Civil War, higher education in the United States had essentially been the preserve of aspiring gentlemen destined for the professions and other leadership positions in society. The land-grant colleges dramatically widened access to higher education to a whole new range of young men and women, to new careers and aspirations. The history of American higher education from then until now has been a steady and continuing widening of access, in response not simply to the nation's general commitment to equality of opportunity but also to a recognition that an increasingly complex society requires educational institutions that are responsive to the urgent demands of new purposes.

As laudable as it may be as an ideal, the widening of access also has contributed to the confusions that have beset the baccalaureate experience. The tension between democratic values and the effort to maintain standards for an undergraduate education can be creative, but too often numbers and political considerations have prevailed over quality and rationality in shaping the undergraduate course of study.

That course of study has been battered by history and by every group that shares an interest in it. Successive generations of students carry differing expectations to the academic enterprise, and they leave their mark. Today's student populations are less well-prepared, more vocationally oriented, and apparently more materialistic than their immediate predecessors. College administrators are required, at the peril of losing their jobs and their institutions, to pay attention to the peculiar characteristics of each generation of students. And they must also, even if reluctantly, admit that for most students the environment in which the curriculum is embedded—the extracurricular activities, the social life, the wide world of the campus—competes with the curriculum for their attention and allegiance. The credential is for most students more important than the course. Therefore, it is critically important for academic institutions to pay more attention than they have to the course for which they are prepared to deliver the credential.

Legislatures and governing boards are so oriented by numbers and money that they and academic administrators neglect energetic scrutiny of their true mission. In the 1960s when higher education was a growth industry, many colleges had little difficulty with growth at the same time that new levels of expectation were supporting a concern for higher quality. But now, with fear of diminishing numbers, drift has taken over. A survival ethic encourages a hunkering down, a diminished vision, whereas a quieter and less dynamic climate should be recognized as providing a marvelous opportunity for renewal, a time for making higher education the vital instrument for enabling generations of young men and women to grasp a vision of the good life, a life of responsible citizenship and human decency.

Our colleges and universities must more than survive their troubles: they must surmount them and put them to creative use, for society expects more of them than in the past. In medicine, law, and engineering, for example, new kinds of problems are inspiring new definitions of appropriate professional training. Governments will reqire recruits to public service prepared to speak long-neglected foreign languages, to comprehend the complexities of changing international relationships, to deal with the challenges of new social and environmental conditions, and to bring to the conduct of urban affairs a new dimension of self-awareness and urgency. None of these needs will be adequately met without a vital transformation in the way our colleges and universities go about their business.

Central to the troubles and to the solution are the professors, for the development that overwhelmed the old curriculum and changed the entire nature of higher education was the transformation of the professors from teachers concerned with the characters and minds of their students to professionals, scholars with Ph.D. degrees with an allegiance to academic disciplines stronger than their commitment to teaching or to the life of the institutions where they are employed. As appropriate as research is as the focus of energies and resources in the research university, the exclusive concern with research in the training of recipients of the Ph.D. degree—to the neglect of any concern with teaching or with any professional responsibility other than to scholarship—has encouraged college faculties to abandon the sense of corporate responsibility that characterized professors of the pre-professional era.

Adept at looking out for themselves—departmental staffing, student enrollments, courses reflecting narrow scholarly interests, attendance at professional meetings—professors unquestionably offer in their courses

6

exquisite examples of specialized learning. But who looks after the shop? Who takes responsibility, not for the needs of the history or English or biology department, but for the curriculum as a whole? Who thinks about the course of study as it is experienced by students? Who reviews and justifies and rationalizes the academic program for which a college awards the coveted credential: a bachelor's degree?

Here the professors and administrators as well are found wanting. Research and specialization, which are what graduate schools are all about, are not all that undergraduate colleges are about. Responsible research and good teaching are compatible, as every college and university can demonstrate, but in the doctoral programs that have certified successive generations of college teachers the balance has been tipped toward research. That bias has entered the ethos of institutions by virtue of the way that professors have been trained and therefore evaluated. Academic leaders, presidents and deans alike, have on the whole failed to combat the dominance of that bias in the undergraduate college, acquiescing in the accumulation of faculty power residing in departments rather than returning faculties to a sense of commitment to the larger responsibilities of their institutions. While curricular incoherence has many causes, some of them all but intractable, the primary means for achieving coherence are bold administrative leaders and newly responsible professors.

The job will not be easy. The extreme individualism of the "do your own thing" ethic, which is an old American value that experienced an especially virulent growth in the 1960s, appears right now to be in remission. Professors and students alike may be ready to respond to some assertion of curricular authority, some definition of what time and wisdom regard as an appropriate baccalaureate experience. On the other hand, a nation as deeply in discord as the United States seems to be will clearly have difficulty in locating shared values and purposes in the undergraduate course of study. In the end, the quality of American life is at stake, the wisdom and humanity of our leaders, our ability as citizens to make informed choices, and the dedication with which we exhibit humane and democratic values as we go about our daily lives.

Higher education shares with other institutions — the schools, churches, media, and professions — a responsibility for how we as a people will meet and shape the future. This generation of academic presidents and deans is required to lead us away from the declining and devalued bachelor's degree that now prevails to a new era of curricular coherence, intellectual rigor, and humanistic strength. Their visions must be bolder, their initiatives more energetic and imaginative, and the great potential for academic leadership that is latent in the authority of their positions must be asserted forcefully and skillfully. Everywhere there are professors eager to join them, waiting only for some sign of executive leadership, some display of concern for the integrity of the college curriculum.

*F*aculty Responsibility: Obstacles and Incentives

Presidents and deans must first confront the obstacles to faculty responsibility that are embedded in academic practice and then, with the cooperation of the professors themselves, fashion a range of incentives to revive the responsibility of the faculty *as a whole* for the curriculum *as a whole.* Every institution has a faculty committee charged with curricular responsibility. These committees have the power to authorize new courses and programs, but they are essentially helpless to design and implement such courses and programs, which necessarily come to them from the departments. The committees themselves are drawn from the departments, which must and do protect their disciplinary turf. Curriculum committees are adept at approving what departments want, skillful at cosmetic tinkering that puts a new and fashionable face on old practices and programs; but except in rare instances and under the prodding of energetic academic leaders, they are seldom innovative. Hardly ever do they consider in any systematic way the curricular structure as a whole or seriously ask whether the curriculum as experienced by a student meets either the institution's defined goals or general goals that are rational, socially healthy, and appropriate.

Faculty curriculum committees suffer from chronic paralysis. They are repositories of great potential power, but they are also pervaded by a great sense of helplessness. Specialized accrediting agencies and professional societies, as well as the examinations for admission to postgraduate professional schools, hover over the curriculum. State departments of education define the high school curriculum and thereby influence what colleges and universities can and cannot do with theirs. In the case of public institutions, state coordinating agencies, as guardians of the educational purse and watchdogs of program duplication, are in a position to overrule faculty decisions. Above all the claim to autonomy by departments, their power to resist unwanted change and to protect their interests, makes serving on a curriculum committee an exercise in frustration and misdirected energy.

An effective curriculum committee should find itself challenging some of the fundamental assumptions and practices of the academy. It should concern itself with the quality of college and university teaching, on which, after all, the effectiveness of any curriculum depends. In doing so it would have to confront the distorted reward system that makes research a

9

more important factor than teaching or even service on the curriculum committee. The value system of the best and brightest products of research universities puts little emphasis on good teaching, counseling of students, and working with secondary schools and secondary school teachers. While this value system is most evident in the research universities, it permeates all of our four-year institutions, imported as part of the baggage that goes with the Ph.D. degree. Research, not teaching, pays off in enhanced reputation, respect of peers beyond one's own campus, and access to funds. The language of the academy is revealing: professors speak of teaching *loads* and research *opportunities,* never the reverse.

A model curriculum committee would, therefore, engage itself in a continuing assessment of the quality of teaching in its institution, even as it sought evidence that such other essential encouragements to learning as libraries and laboratories were also in good health. It would possess the wisdom to acknowledge that a college or university faculty is a repository of powerful conflicting ideologies and political views seeking expression in the course of study, but it would also have the will to keep the institution's curricular structure and goals from being bent out of shape by a too ready acquiescence in the ambitions of every faculty special interest. It would find ways to celebrate superb teaching, of which there is much, and draw attention to successful teaching practices that are capable of broader applications. It would walk a fine line between the demands of the local community, the state, regional business and industrial interests, and

other representatives of the external community and the demands of its own understanding of what a coherent undergraduate program should be: it would be responsive *and* resistant.

The curriculum committee would become the most intellectually exciting and challenging committee on campus. It would address central issues, bring to the surface long-neglected concerns, and create a new partnership in learning between students, long afflicted by a curriculum that has not taken itself or their needs as seriously as should be, and professors, far too long comfortably protected from responsibility by history, paralysis, timid academic leaders, and the narrow training and value system that has denied to college teaching appropriate professional standards and expectations.

Surely the disarray that now prevails is not a measure of the wisdom of American college professors on curricular matters. They can do better, and it is in their interest to do so. Any further and continuing confusion of purpose in the curriculum can only lead to public disaffection, a withdrawal of support, and a demand for greater accountability enforced by external agencies. The long-term interests of the professors transcend the short-term individual interests that have them scrambling for grants, peer support, promotion, and tenure. In the end, the health of higher education and the viability of the curriculum will determine whether those symbols of individual success are worth having.

For all of the pervasiveness of the conventional reward system, there is deep disquiet within the academy. Many faculty give only grudging acquiescence to a system that puts the highest premium on research and publication. There is considerable discontent among the professors themselves with the quality of teaching generally; most of them welcome signals of seriousness about teaching and are willing to acknowledge that something important was missing in their graduate school education. For while all of them were prepared to be professional economists or physicists or whatever, none was prepared for the profession of undergraduate teaching, for the ethical standards and levels of performance appropriate to the responsibility of being not only the professor of a subject but a college teacher.

The graduate school model, with its single-minded focus on the preparation for research, serves as the standard by which colleges and universities everywhere judge themselves. In the long run nothing less than the reconstruction of the training of college teachers and a revision of prevailing standards in the recruitment of faculty will liberate the curriculum and the professors themselves from a misguided overemphasis on research and a corresponding neglect of teaching. The enemy of good teaching is not research, but rather the spirit that says that this is the only worthy or legitimate task for faculty members. An emphasis on teaching, moreover, does not require the denigration of research. The finest teachers are often the best researchers. Imparting to students some sense of the wonders, complexities, ambiguities, and uncertainties that accompany the experience of learning and growing can and often should be intimately connected with the dissemination of new knowledge. But teaching comes first. This message must be forcefully delivered by academic leaders responsible for undergraduate education to the research universities that have awarded the Ph.D. degree to generation after generation of potential professors professionally unprepared to teach.

In an environment that is serious about the quality of teaching, the grand design of the curriculum will receive the attention that it deserves. What can be done to encourage American college professors to revive their corporate responsibility to the curriculum? How can they be inspired to reinvigorate the curriculum, making it an expression not of their special disciplinary interests but of their considered judgment of what a baccalaureate education ought to be? Sabbatical leaves, now given as a matter of routine or in expectation of research results, could also be given for the kind of professional development that would result in improved teaching. Professional leaves could be provided for individual or group projects designed to encourage the systematic improvement of teaching. Funds could be earmarked and awarded on a competitive basis for projects explicitly developed for improved teaching, course design, and curricular reform. One or all of these encouragements now exist in some institutions, but they are not yet anywhere so habitual and well-funded as to constitute the bold assault on the graduate school/ research ethos that is so pervasive.

A faculty task force on curriculum development and experimentation, drawn from across the faculty and rewarded with released time, might be asked to explore what is currently known about learning and what practices have been developed that best support a congenial atmosphere for teaching and learning. Such an exploration would be a novel experience for all but some of the psychologists on undergraduate faculties as they have now been trained.

A new area of research, still in its infancy, has been evolving during the last decade. It arose and is still rooted in the natural sciences. It is directed toward understanding how students learn (or fail to learn) specific subject matter, what difficulties they have with various modes of abstract logical reasoning, what preconceptions or misconceptions impede their mastery of concepts or principles in the given subject, what instructional approaches and devices are effective in helping learners overcome the obstacles which are encountered, what exercises and feed-back accelerate the development of various desirable skills, and how best to make use of new instructional technology.

We refer not to psychological research—which has had little or no impact on teaching in other disciplines—but to research indigenous to specific subject areas, such as physics—research having results that can be readily understood and directly applied by teachers of the subject. Such research could and should be conducted in disciplines other than the natural sciences, and wide application of the insights thus gained into teaching and learning could have a dramatic impact on all of undergraduate education. Research of this kind has, in general, not been successfully conducted in either psychology or education departments because it requires deep, expert knowledge of specific subject matter. If departments, particularly research departments, allocated one or two regular faculty positions to research on learning their discipline, they could produce results which would improve their own teaching effectiveness and would have visibility and impact beyond the walls of their own institutions. They would influence instructional materials at the secondary as well as the college level. And they could educate young researchers who would continue the enterprise and propagate it to institutions where it does not yet exist.

We believe that on every campus there can be assembled for productive work faculty members who care deeply about good teaching and about a curriculum that would give substance, vitality, and coherence to undergraduate education. No curriculum can assert itself as a fixed definition of truth. It must be responsive to the changing needs and expectations of society and to intellectual social changes that alter our definitions of reality. The curriculum must be under constant examination and assessment, as vulnerable to pruning as open to growth. Faculty members charged with major responsibility for that examination must learn to discriminate between what their colleagues would like to teach and what makes sense as a significant experience in learning for students and as a contribution to the overall design and structure of the curriculum. It is a central obligation of college and university administrations to create the supports necessary to make such a faculty group a vehicle of institutional integrity and purpose.

Professors must be encouraged to escape the confines of departments without penalty. Team teaching in another department, honors programs that bring together faculty in such a way as to make their contributions to the learning experience of their students more than a sum of their separate roles, budget allocations favoring interdisciplinary efforts, appointments of both short and longer duration of professors not to departments but to divisions — these are some of the ways in which academic administrators can alter the ways in which their faculties fulfill their responsibilities to the curriculum. Another way would be to create well-paid professorships to which would be appointed highly qualified teacher-scholars with a demonstrated capacity for imaginative interdisciplinary humanistic teaching. These professors would not be assigned to departments or divisions: they would be community assets.

Loosening some of the grip of academic departments on curricular arrangements is an attractive prospect. On the other hand, a rigid hostility to the contribution of external groups to the academic enterprise can be a barrier to effective reform. There are many opportunities for imaginative and constructive interaction with the world beyond the campus. Trustees and graduates are a natural link with business, industry, government, the arts, and the professions, those segments of society that attract a substantial portion of the nation's talent. Surely there are creative ways to enrich the baccalaureate experience by tapping these resources beyond the campus. The writer or artist in residence concept has been successful in breaking down the restraints of traditional programs and practices, but too often such appointments have been token nods in the direction of creativity in environments more conditioned and congenial to a hard-nosed respect for academic scholarship. Professors in residence could be drawn from the entire firmament of the external world, especially from the newly retired and from those temporarily available for such assignments.

Colleges that have made experimental use of such outsiders in their one-month winter programs have been pleasantly surprised at the curricular enrichment they contribute and at their success as teachers, although candor would have to allow that the outsiders have been teaching in their spheres for many years, with no less formal training in how to teach than that of the professors themselves. These same external resources could be exploited in creating work-study programs, career education programs, and internships in government and business, and other experiences that unite rather than oppose the values of career and of liberal learning.

General faculty discontent with the curriculum is not likely to lead to a spontaneous assault on the conditions that generate unrest. Inertia is the style with which faculties move from day to day, from year to year. Presidents, academic vice-presidents, and deans have the fundamental obligation to identify the curricular issues that require attention and to shape a strategy to move their faculties to responsible action. They must reassert leadership in curricular matters, a responsibility allowed to weaken while the material concerns of their institutions developed into an almost exclusive preoccupation. Academic leaders must help faculty transform their "propensity to veto into an inclination to initiate," as it was so aptly put by the General Secretary of the AAUP in his 1984 report to the membership. Where in recent years the presidents and deans have taken a lead in setting up task forces for deep review of such questions as general education and admission requirements, higher education has moved responsibly and imaginatively toward confronting its crisis. But where administrators have failed to take the initiative, the crisis grows. Many serious faculty members have given these and other questions informed, sometimes institutionally productive thought, not always in log-rolling ways. They have needed supportive administrators in order to be effective.

Boards of trustees hold in trust, in law and in fact, the destiny of higher education in the United States. For a variety of reasons, including the ascendancy of the professional professors in the power structure and the role of the president as chief executive officer, trustees have spent most of their energies on the material interests of the colleges and universities, on matters of investment, land, buildings, budget, and management. Academic issues have become either peripheral for them or "off limits." It is not necessary for trustees to tread into sacred faculty territory—academic freedom, tenure, the selection of texts—in order to be responsible to their trust. But they must ask searching questions about whether academic programs are of high quality and consonant with their institutions'

mission. A board that fails to provide itself with frequent and thorough review of key curricular issues is neglecting its duties, for one of those duties is to make sure that the faculties do not neglect theirs.

Faculties, administrators, and trustees have a collective responsibility to their institutions and their students. It is a corporate responsibility that can be carried out effectively and imaginatively only if the respective roles are carefully defined and only if each group recognizes that, in the end, its role is to educate students who for a time pass under their joint nurture. The board must oversee. The presidents and their assistants must lead. The faculty must face and live with the substantive issues. In the end, however, the performance of the faculty will decide whether the integrity of the curriculum will be restored.

A Minimum Required Curriculum

Our message to administrators and professors alike is that the curriculum requires structure, a framework sturdier than simply a major and general distribution requirements and more reliable than student interest. We do not believe that concern for coverage and factual knowledge is where the construction of a curriculum should begin. We propose a minimum required program of study for all students, consisting of the intellectual, aesthetic, and philosophic experiences that should enter into the lives of men and women engaged in baccalaureate education. We *do not* believe that the road to a coherent undergraduate education can be constructed from a set of required subjects or academic disciplines. We *do* believe that there are methods and processes, modes of access to understanding and judgment, that should inform all study. While learning cannot of course take place devoid of subject matter, how that subject matter is experienced is what concerns us here. We are in search of an education that will enable the American people to live responsibly and joyfully, fulfilling their promise as individual humans and their obligations as democratic citizens. We believe that the following nine experiences are essential to that kind of education: some of them might be thought of as skills, others as ways of growing and understanding; we think that *all* of them are basic to a coherent undergraduate education.

1. *Inquiry, abstract logical thinking, critical analysis.* How do we know? Why do we believe? What is the evidence? Here, whatever the subject matter, we are at the heart of the intellectual process, concerned with the phenomenon of humans thinking, the processes whereby they establish a fact, put two or more of them together, come to conclusions as to their meaning, and perhaps even soar with some leap of imagination to a thought that has never been thought before. To reason well, to recognize when reason and evidence are not enough, to discover the legitimacy of intuition, to subject inert data to the probing analysis of the mind — these are the primary experiences required of the undergraduate course of study. There is not a subject taught nor a discipline entrenched in the curriculum that should fail to provide students with a continuing practice in thinking of the kind we here discuss. Probably most of us, inside and outside the academic community, assume that if anything is paid attention to in our colleges and universities, thinking

15

must be it. Unfortunately, thinking can be lazy. It can be sloppy. It can be reactive rather than active. It can be inert. It can be fooled, misled, bullied. In colleges and universities it is all of these things, as well as perceptive, deep, imaginative, careful, quick, and clever. Students possess great untrained and untapped capacities for logical thinking, critical analysis, and inquiry, but these are capacities that are not spontaneous: they grow out of wise instruction, experience, encouragement, correction, and constant use.

2. *Literacy: writing, reading, speaking, listening.* Literacy is a heavy word, a concept so full of meaning that it is often misused to mean more and less than it does. For us, writing, as literacy, means being in possession of language, knowing its shapes and possibilities, being so accustomed to its grammar and rules that the why is unnecessary, always aware that writing is an expression of thinking, a give-away of how we think and feel and judge. Writing can be effusive, stiff, controlled, explosive; it is always revealing of what lies behind it. Since a baccalaureate education is intended to lead young men and women to a satisfying possession of themselves, then writing should lead them there. Clarity, directness, simplicity even in the ordering of complicated ideas, originality, and playful fun in the use of words — these are some of the goals that should guide students in their experience with writing as an exercise in literacy.

Now that television is a fundamental agency of education in the United States reading is not as central to becoming literate as it once was. Television is a presence, a teacher, a guide to word sounds, style, and ways of saying things. It is also in a hurry: contemplation, deep thought, is not what it is about. Reading is something else again. It is an experience with others, with the way others put words together to reveal how they think and perhaps how they want us to think. Reading is a conduit to critical thinking.

Reading is an invitation to take time to spend time with someone else somewhere else. There are many ways to read, and college students should have many opportunities to experience the best ways. They know how to read in a hurry or to read when they don't want to; they can read tired, drugged, and haphazardly. But they need to be taught how to read actively, arguing along the way with every word and assertion; and how to read aesthetically and critically, seeking the word, the expression, the exact form of phrase or direction that catches the reader just when the reader wants to escape — reading in order to write better.

Reading is for finding out, for discovering the fun of thinking, analysis, and inquiry. All reading in college and university courses is not like that; all cannot be, but more must be. Indeed, we urge our colleagues to allow for more reading, those structured invitations to contemplation and self-education that characterize memorable undergraduate courses, and fewer lectures, those invitations to passivity and pencil-pushing that are generally, although certainly not always, educationally counterproductive.

Speaking is another aspect of literacy. We are a century and more away from the time when going to college meant instruction in oratory, stage presence, debate, and the arts of oral persuasion. Television talk shows, political campaigns, and news broadcasts have taken their place. They are miserable examples and worse teachers. In the meantime, speeches have to be given, memoranda written, directions understood. The world's work needs to be done, and as it becomes more complex, it needs to be conveyed and described and comprehended in language that is clear, simple, and to-the-point. Listening itself is a function of literacy. Students should become adept at listening creatively, recognizing the uses to which language is put, anticipating the drift of a speaker's thought, identifying the vacuous and the perceptive.

Television is so much a part of our lives that it is foolish simply to deplore its weaknesses and its bad habits. Students need to learn how to look at and listen to their television sets critically, with as much focused intellectual energy as they are expected to apply to other experiences that call on their ability to listen and see intelligently.

Not every word or combination of words, whether read or written or spoken, can be expressions of unassailable style, models of taste and beauty that will endure. Some of us are better at these things than others, but none of us should be given up for lost. There are pleasures in sharing human excellence, even while trying and failing to be the best. A bachelor's degree should mean that its holders can read, write, and speak at levels of distinction and have been given many opportunities to learn how. It also should mean that many of them do so with style.

3. *Understanding numerical data.* We have become a society bombarded by numbers. We are threatened by them. We are intimidated by them. We are lied to with their help. We are comforted by them and seduced by them. They tell us our chances of getting cancer if we smoke. They tell us who we are going to vote for and why. They tell us whether we are poor or rich, whether to carry our umbrellas, how to invest. The interpretation of numerical data requires a sophisticated level of understanding and there is no reason to expect that the situation will become any less pressing. We are not here proposing a new subject for the curriculum, but we are arguing for a recognition throughout the course of study of the necessity for sharpening the ability of students to understand numerical data, to recognize their misuse, the multiple interpretations they often permit, and the ways that they can be manipulated to mislead.

At the same time students must be made aware of the ways in which numerical data increasingly make accessible levels of knowledge and understanding not possible for earlier generations. Quantitative research in history is recovering the lives of people once imbedded in tax lists and forgotten census returns. Counting the use of certain key words in an "author unknown" essay can lead to an informed attribution. The computer, fed the appropriate numbers, can imagine the future and assist in institutional planning, inventory control, the projection of traffic patterns and tax revenues. Numbers are not neutral. They are not inert. They are as alive as we are when they greet us and we greet them: they become what we understand them to be. For that reason, in a world of numbers students should encounter concepts that permit a sophisticated response to arguments and positions which depend on numbers and statistics. Such concepts would include degree of risk, scatter, uncertainty, orders of magnitude, rates of change, confidence levels and acceptability, and the interpretation of graphs as they are manifest in numbers. Citizens intellectually comfortable with these concepts would, among other things, be less vulnerable to the misuse of numbers by advertisers and political candidates. They would, for example, know the difference between a current dollar and a dollar of constant value.

4. *Historical consciousness.* We carry within ourselves the seeds of historical consciousness and experience: we grow older and know that we were younger; we have a history. So does everyone and everything else. The more refined our historical understanding, the better prepared we are to recognize complexity, ambiguity, and uncertainty as intractable conditions of human society. The student with a sharply honed historical consciousness knows that everything is not what it seems to be, that what should be a simple solution to a simple problem will not work because unexpressed historical forces and traditions lie just beneath the surface waiting to be awakened. Such a student does not believe everything read, becomes a cautious skeptic, learns to recognize that events occur sequentially, and that the sequence matters. A consciousness of history allows us to impose some intellectual order on the disorder of random facts. It invites the application of abstract logical thinking, critical analysis, and inquiry to the past, but it also requires imagination and intuition if the past is going to make sense. Facts do not speak for themselves: meaning must be drawn from them by minds soundly trained, nurtured to recognize their opportunities, experienced in making the connections and grasping the complexities that history piles up around us. Historical consciousness helps to make the world comprehensible.

If everyone and everything has a history, then the opportunities for nurturing historical consciousness in a baccalaureate program are manifestly unlimited. That does not mean, however, that historical consciousness just comes naturally, nor that it can be delivered on order by the history department in large survey courses or in textbook assignments in narrative histories. History is all over the course of study—in the languages, art, music, literatures, social studies, the sciences, and in history itself. The best way to develop historical consciousness is to study historical situations in depth, whether the situation is the emergence of a school of painting, the outbreak of a war, the critical reception of a major writer, the adoption of certain economic policies, the appearance of a new educational movement, or the evolution of a new scientific insight deepening our view of man's place in the universe. The use of primary materials—the documents, the letters, diaries, contemporary accounts, visual remains, biographies, the scores of places where history resides—will disabuse any student of the harmful notion that life is a simple process of cause and effect. To exercise historical consciousness is to stretch the mind and to avoid the pitfalls of oversimplification, shallowness, and unexamined and unchallenged evidence.

5. *Science.* In his celebrated effort to make the world comprehensible and manageable, Henry Adams turned his autobiographical wanderings, *The Education of Henry Adams,* into an intellectual tour of the nineteenth century. Acknowledging that science had unleashed great energies that man showed little readiness or ability to understand or to control, he concluded that what was needed was nothing less than a new, self-conscious intellectual style that was equal to the challenges that he located symbolically in the dynamos that captured his imagination at the great expositions in Chicago in 1893 and Paris in 1900. "Thus far," Adams concluded, "since five or ten thousand years, the mind had successfully reacted, and nothing yet proved that it would fail to react — but it would need to jump." Adams equipped for himself a mind that jumped, fashioning tools of analysis and attitudes of mind—observation, intuition, skepticism, a sense of paradox and ambiguity, a sense of proportion, even of beauty and value— into a most remarkable instrument for analyzing his world. He was not a scientist, but he understood the scientist's style.

We are now more than half a century from Adams' troubled observation that humanity little understood or controlled the energies that science had unleashed. In the meantime those energies have leveled Hiroshima, given us acid rain, and placed men on the moon and a personal computer on every desk. The energies accelerate, the understanding and control lag. If it is not possible to be altogether comfortable in the contemporary world, surely the world is less bewildering to someone who understands the nature of science, its methods, its reliability, and its limitations. Scientific truths are as vulnerable to revision as any other truths, but the scientist's way of reaching truths consists of methods that lead from truth to truth, with yesterday's truth discarded as no longer valid where new knowledge and understandings lead.

A person who understands what science is recognizes that scientific concepts are created by acts of human intelligence and imagination; comprehends the distinction between observation and inference and between the occasional role of accidental discovery in scientific investigation and the deliberate strategy of forming and testing hypotheses; understands how theories are formed, tested, validated, and accorded provisional acceptance; and discriminates between conclusions that rest on unverified assertion and those that are developed from the application of scientific reasoning.

To be intellectually at ease with science is to understand, too, the limitations that are inherent in scientific inquiry, the kinds of questions that science neither asks nor answers. A comprehensive understanding of science also requires awareness of the ways in which scientific knowledge has had direct impact on intellectual history and on one's own view of the universe and of the human condition, as well as awareness of how certain modes of thought in natural science — forming concepts, testing hypotheses, discriminating between observation and inference, constructing models — inform such disciplines as history, economics, sociology, and political science. The kind of scientific understanding that is here described has thus far eluded most Americans, including holders of the bachelor's degree.

A student can best take possession of science and its methods not in a broad course about science but in a course where the subject matter is highly circumscribed, even narrow. With skillful teaching, in discussions of primary research papers on a single problem in a subdivision of science students can be led to examine skeptically the relationships asserted between data and conclusions, to suggest alternative hypotheses, and to design new laboratory procedures that may test further the conclusions drawn. Consideration of such methodological problems can in turn be used to raise philosophic questions about the nature of science and the influence of political values or social setting on scientific research. One promising approach to the study of science is interdisciplinary. Properly structured and taught, interdisciplinary science courses would focus on concepts and enigmas, provide introductory training for students intending to concentrate in the scientific disciplines, satisfy the need of all bachelor's candidates for scientific understanding, and thus permit revolution in the standard pre-medical science requirements.

The kind of experience with science that we here describe is intended to make the American college graduate a less helpless bystander of a world made by science. By demystifying science, to some extent emphasizing the human, social, and political implications of scientific research, such study should lead students to greater resiliency and a greater sense of their own capacity to play a role in how the results of science are used. And certainly in the laboratory they will learn how to observe, experiment, and infer, and catch on to the importance of observation — paying attention with imagination and concentration — in the sequence of learning.

6. *Values.* Unquestionably suspended judgment is the appropriate mode of scientific inquiry; it allows investigation to proceed and postpones decision until evidence requires it. But men and women do not live in suspension. They must make real choices, assume responsibility for their decisions, be comfortable with their own behavior and know why. They must embody the values of a democratic society in order to fulfill the responsibilities of citizenship. They must be equipped to be perceptive and wise critics of that society, repositories of the values that make civilized and humane society possible.

After a hundred years as capstone of the curriculum, the senior course in moral philosophy disappeared at the end of the nineteenth century. It had supplanted theology as the source and definition of values in the course of study, just as it would be supplanted by so-called value-free social science and objective science. In the moral philosophy course students investigated "the sources of moral behavior as well as the nature of virtue itself," assured by their teachers, usually the college presidents, that reason and human nature would lead them to goodness. A remarkable and far-ranging excursion into social and individual ethics, the moral philosophy course sent young graduates out into the world with a reassuring sense of their own fitness to play a role in the moral order.

A dozen discrete subjects—among them sociology, psychology, economics, and political science—spilled out of the old moral philosophy course in the late nineteenth century, in effect announcing that no longer could a liberal education rest on a belief in the unity of knowledge. But more than the unity of knowledge fell out of the curriculum. While ethical concern and social responsibility inspired many of the early social science courses, questions of value and moral character were increasingly shunted aside, as the course of study and its professionally trained practitioners were oriented toward the values of scientific investigation. In the end, almost everywhere the only certain place in the curriculum where human values and character received attention was in the ethics course of the philosophy department, where, although rigorous analysis could lead to choice and responsiblity, the experience was available for only a few students.

There is no place in the course of study where the capacity to make informed and responsible moral choice cannot appropriately be nurtured. We may be wary of final answers, but we cannot avoid the necessity of choice, decision, judgment. The curricular opportunities are legion: Abraham Lincoln willing to accept a constitutional amendment protecting slavery in the South in order to frustrate secession; Captain Vere wrestling with complex issues of innocence and justice, good and evil, in *Billy Budd*; the tension between neighborhood and urban renewal in the city of your choice; Who owns the Elgin marbles?; equity in the tax structure; barriers to voter registration, immigration, and imports; Vietnam, Iran, Grenada—the choices and the values; Holocaust—evil and guilt; Los Alamos—a scientific community in the real world; an inquiry into human tragedy in literature; crime and punishment.

The opportunities are there, but they are too seldom taken by teachers so far gone into specialization and into the scientific understanding of their specialties that the challenges of bringing students into humanistic relationship with their subjects, into the arena of values and choice and judgment, are beyond their interest and capacity. Recruiting teachers with a professional commitment to teaching may be one way to focus subject matter on life, its quality, the agonies and joys, the demands and choices of growing up.

7. *Art.* Appreciation and experience of the fine and performing arts are as essential as any other qualities appropriate to a civilized human being and a democratic society. In 1780, in one of those quiet moments that a busy life allowed him, John Adams, then engaged in a diplomatic mission in Europe, reflected: "I must study politics and war that my sons may have liberty to study mathematics and philosophy. My sons ought to study mathematics and philosophy, geography, natural history and naval architecture, in order to give their children a right to study painting, poetry, music, architecture, statuary, tapestry and porcelain." Adams' time-

table for the arrival of the arts as college studies was off by several generations; his great-grandsons (let alone his grandsons) finished their Harvard studies between 1856 and 1870 without formal exposure to the arts. A century and several generations later the arts can no longer be denied access to the curriculum nor relegated to a peripheral position. They are therefore to be encouraged as providing access to realms of creativity, imagination, and feeling that explore and enlarge the meaning of what it is to be human.

The languages of art, music, architecture, drama, and dance open up new worlds of human endeavor and communication, of truth and of representation. We find ourselves in that special environment where means and ends are the same, where sensibilities and sensitivities otherwise dormant within us are called forth, announcing their arrival with perceptions, feelings, and empathies we did not know we possessed. Without a knowledge of the language of the fine arts, we see less and hear less. Without some experience in the performing arts we are denied the knowledge of disciplined creativity and its meaning as a bulwark of freedom and an instrument of social cohesion.

Trained eyes and ears enlarge the environment, join forces with reason, intuition, and a sense of history in recognizing the ways in which the Sistine Chapel, a Wagnerian opera, a Japanese floral arrangement, a Rembrandt portrait, and breakdancing are expressions both of exuberant individual creativity and of the culture that nurtured them. Once more we are led to a sense of the complexities and interrelationships of human society, a sense of the values that inform artistic expression and performance. As John Adams intended, we become less barbaric, more civilized, more fit to be the standard-bearers of a vibrant democratic society.

8. *International and multicultural experiences.* Any subject, if presented liberally, will take students into a world beyond themselves, make them again and again outsiders, so that they may return and know themselves better. All study is intended to break down the narrow certainties and provincial vision with which we are born. In a sense, we are all from the provinces, including New Yorkers and Bostonians, whose view of the world can be as circumscribed as that of native Alaskans who have never left their village. To broaden the horizons of understanding for men and women, therefore, colleges must provide them with access to the diversity of cultures and experiences that define American society and the contemporary world

Ethnic diversity in the United States has supported rich traditions of architecture, cuisine, humor, political allegiance, and family customs. There are class cultures, cultures of place and gender and profession—a culture of poverty, of the farm, of the rural South and the urban ghetto. Japan and China, the aspiring peoples of Africa, the troubled nations of Central and South America, the Soviet Union and its satellites, and the countries of Western Europe with which we share the values and inheritance of Western Civilization —here are the resources for the study of human cultures, the differences that define particular group identities and the common experiences that make them expressions of human possibility.

How should a college go about opening the eyes and minds of its students to the shrinking world in which they live and to the aspirations of women and of the ethnic minorities who are redefining American social and political reality? There are opportunities in many of the solidly entrenched disciplines of the curriculum to widen access to the diversity of American and world cultures. The study of foreign language and literature can be enriched by exploring the culture of which it is an artifact. In recent years, American history courses have discovered black Americans and women and in the process made history itself more meaningful. The art and literature of Africa and Asia are breaking into courses of study once tied almost exclusively to the Western world. Programs of study in foreign countries are increasingly popular, less because colleges are enthusiastic about them than because students sense that a term abroad offers great opportunities for intellectual growth and understanding with lifelong dividends. A comparable motivation inspired an earlier generation of young American college graduates to enter the Peace Corps and allowed upper class English families to provide their sons with an extended tour of Europe as a finishing course in their education. The fragility of the world in which we live and the volatile diversity of the population of the United States adds urgency to the need for international and multicultural experience in the course of study. At this moment in history colleges are not being asked to produce village squires but citizens of a shrinking world and a changing America. Colleges must create a curriculum in which the insights and understandings, the lives and aspirations of the distant and foreign, the different and the neglected, are more widely comprehended by their graduates.

9. *Study in depth.* The minimum required curriculum that we here propose does not consist of required courses or prescribed subjects. Our concern is what happens to students when they study subjects and take courses in the various academic disciplines. Our focus is the methods and processes, the modes of access to understanding and judgment, that shape their formal undergraduate education. One experience that students should have is study in depth, concentration in a discipline or group of disciplines, that conveys both the possibilities and the limits of such study. We will address in greater detail elsewhere in this report what study in depth should and should not be. Here we want only to argue in behalf of the experience.

Students bound from course to course, year to year, lecture hall to lecture hall, term paper to term paper, quiz to quiz, participating in an unending, they sometimes feel, series of discrete educational events. They are learning, for sure. Ideally, their minds are instruments of logic, critical analysis, and inquiry. They are learning to read, write, and speak with clarity and style. Numbers neither baffle nor trick them, but instead inform their understanding and enlarge the range of their minds. They know that everything has a past, including the thoughts they have just expressed. Scientific method is leading them to be better observers and more willing to acknowledge that learning involves a sequence of observations, connections, and conclusions. They are confronting their humanity in many ways—in the inescapability of moral choice and responsibility, in the joy of art both appreciated and performed, and in access to the diverse worlds beyond the families and neighborhoods that they know best. Education in depth, however, is an experience in learning of a different order.

Depth requires sequential learning, building on blocks of knowledge that lead to more sophisticated understanding and encourage leaps of the imagination and efforts at synthesis. Depth is achieved through a variety of experiences that broaden the student's knowledge of a discipline, strengthening analytical powers while leading to a deeper, fresher, more complex perspective. Depth requires the kind of focused inquiry that takes time; it releases students to the testing of their own skills; it should not be hurried. The year-long essay, the senior thesis, the artistic project, undertaken after a sound grasp of the fundamentals of the discipline or art has been established, provides an experience in which two great lessons are learned: the joy of mastery, the thrill of moving forward in a formal body of knowledge and gaining some effective control over it, integrating it, perhaps even making some small contribution to it; and the lesson that no matter how deeply and widely students dig, no matter how much they know, they cannot know enough, they cannot

know everything. Depth is an enemy of arrogance.

In proposing this minimum required curriculum, consisting of nine criteria or objectives that should define the learning of every college undergraduate, we clearly have placed our emphasis on how to learn. The distinction between ways of knowing and knowledge is a false one—there can be no knowing without knowledge because knowing leads there. On the other hand, knowledge can be served up and passed around without regard for the ways of knowing. The problem with the American college curriculum is not that it has failed to offer up knowledge. The problem is that it offers too much knowledge with too little attention to how that knowledge has been created and what methods and styles of inquiry have led to its creation. The skills and experience of our minimum required curriculum deny the distinction. There are ways of knowing that are also invitations to knowledge and to a shared culture. We propose that faculties focus on the "how" and allow their sense of what is essential and appropriate to a common culture to shape the selection of the "what." The result will be not only a pruning of the curriculum but also an enrichment of its content.

The nine elements of our minimum course of study do not add up to an invitation to establish prescribed survey courses in literature and science, nor do they suggest solving the curricular problems of higher education by simply strengthening distribution requirements or adding multidisciplinary general education courses. We believe that either one of these old solutions is more likely to perpetuate than to remedy the conditions that brought our committee into existence. Both of them are comfortably appealing, for they do not challenge the ways in which power and responsibility have been used in the past. They substitute coverage for teaching and learning.

Nowhere do we say that there is only one way to gain access to the diverse cultures that define the contemporary world and shape American society. We see no reason to impose a *course* on understanding numerical data on every student. By the same token, there is no defensible reason why English departments should alone bear the responsibility for literacy in the American college and university. Writing across the curriculum is a common sense concept that expresses what an undergraduate education should offer in the realm of training for literacy: many opportunities to write in all courses, serious attention to written work by instructors in all courses, a variety of writing experiences—short papers, long papers, quick papers, unhurried papers, reports, critiques, narratives. Like writing, other avenues to literacy —reading and speaking and listening —should find outlets and encouragement across the curriculum. So, too, with critical analysis, inquiry, understanding numerical data, values, and historical consciousness.

While science and art can find comfortable lodging in courses other than those offered in the scientific disciplines and in the fine and performing arts, it is probable that at this stage in the history of American higher education the goals we seek under the headings of *Science* and *Art* will be best realized in particular courses rather than, as might be ideal, across the curriculum. The training of college professors, either in their undergraduate years or in graduate school, does not yet allow for that exalted level of general learning.

In every way our proposals are an invitation to a greater respect for students, an enhanced responsibility for the quality of teaching, and a fundamental concern for the qualities of mind and character to be nurtured by a coherent education. How might an institution go about structuring our proposed minimum required program of study? Habit is so ingrained a mode of action—or inaction —in the colleges and universities that it is almost impossible to imagine how to operate without divisions of the curriculum (usually three) to which disciplines are assigned. Then, once the divisions are settled upon, often for political rather than intellectual reasons, it is a simple matter to require every student to take a prescribed number of courses in each division. The process is known as "distribution": what the courses deliver in the way of intellectual experience is of less importance than the variety of disciplines and subjects that show up on a student's transcript. There has to be a better way.

Although divisions and departments may be convenient and effective instruments for rationalizing the academic enterprise, they are not necessarily synonymous with curricular wisdom. If divisions and departments are so well entrenched in our practices as to be invulnerable, there is no reason why they cannot be charged with redesigning old courses and designing new ones that are responsible to the goals and experiences of the minimum required program that we propose. Structure is not the issue here. Responsibility is.

Equally important are the context and style of these educational experiences. The integrity of a college requires more than a curriculum that looks "right" on paper. The curriculum requires support, an environment in which the priorities of the college actively encourage the realization of the learning desired. The quality of the environment can be measured by emphasis on opportunities for active learning and by evidence that students and faculty are engaged in a joint enterprise of discovery and growth. The prevailing spirit of pedagogy should reduce the possibilities for passivity in students and authoritarianism in faculties. Students should undertake a variety of pedagogical approaches—seminars, lectures, research, field study, tutorials, theses. Every students' program should be guided by informed faculty advice and supervision: perfunctory advising must give way to careful and continuous monitoring and counseling. Imaginative planning, in which administrative funding and student contributions would be essential, could integrate the course of study with the extracurriculum and the cultural environment in many rewarding ways, with particular concern in large urban institutions for the needs of commuting students.

No faculty has yet fully exploited the technological developments—film, video, computer—that will ease the burden of making their courses as widely effective as our minimum required curriculum would allow.

Nor have many institutions fully implemented and encouraged the possibilities for integrating community service, political participation, and other opportunities for civic responsibility with the curricular program. While there are faculties and institutions conscientiously trying to implement these and other promising educational possibilities—and indeed making impressive headway—all colleges and universities, including the best, have a long way to go before they can say that they have established a community of learning.

*S*tudy in Depth

In its origins the traditional major that now prevails in our colleges and universities was a happy alternative to a curricular landscape wholly populated with introductory survey courses. Protected from superficiality by prerequisites and sequence, it conveyed a sense of depth and mastery, as well as the unfortunate illusion that, for instance, a history major that omitted the history of most of the world and concerned itself largely with the dynasties and wars of Western Europe nonetheless covered all the history worth knowing. "Coverage" is no longer possible; historians do not agree on what a history major should be or do; and while many new subjects and methods have entered the history curriculum, the patterns of sequence and pre-. requisites that once helped to deliver depth and mastery have been abandoned. The major in history no longer rests on the justification that gave it birth. The same is largely true throughout the central disciplines of the arts and sciences, while majors in vocational and professional fields are overdetermined by ends other than education.

At a time when the major as it has developed should be under critical review and evaluation, majors have instead been proliferating, especially in the vocational and technical fields, where the appeal of jobs has blinded institutions and students to the ephemeral nature of much that is contained in the new majors. In the meantime, students are being short-changed, denied the intellectual experiences that will enable them to comprehend their world and to live in it freely, courageously, happily, and responsibly. Neither the old majors, weakened and robbed of their original justification, nor the new majors provide the kind of learning that we mean by study in depth.

Today's majors are not so much experiences in depth as they are bureaucratic conveniences: they allow the professors to indulge their professional preoccupations and they allow the deans to control the flow of student traffic. Majors have deflected attention from the serious business of creating an intellectual environment that makes a central concern the quest for the powers of informed judgment and for the dual capacities of appreciation and criticism.

The difficult enterprise of making interpretive decisions and facing up to their full consequences ought to inform each and every course, each and every object of study. From our viewpoint the fundamentals of a college education are the skills attendant upon the understanding of particular interpretations, the power to make decisions among interpretations, and the ability to translate one interpretation in terms of another. "What then is the practice of the academic disciplines?" asks Thomas F. Green, the philosopher of education, in the Summer 1982 issue of *Liberal Education*. "It is the practice of inquiry,. . . actively aimed at satisfying the human desire to know." For Green, as for us, a discipline implies its own virtues —"attend to fact, watch the argument, beware of certainty, beware of possible objections." Mastery of subject matter may be essential to the mastery of an academic discipline, but the discipline—the inquiry—is what leads to knowledge.

Baccalaureate education is argument about interpretations. Little about the major as now constituted is essential to this goal and much about it is detrimental. Too often subject matter and coverage have been allowed to get in the way of sophisticated practice of the disciplines themselves. The curriculum needs to be liberated from the constraints on learning that have been imposed upon it by the traditional major.

Study in depth, if it is to be disciplined and complex, cannot be restricted to the offerings of one academic department. History is almost everywhere in the curriculum: to limit a history concentration to history department courses may serve the ambitions of a department but will certainly deny students the strengthening of their study in depth with a course in the history of English literature, the art of the Renaissance, or a history of economic thought—all

offered outside the department. Breaking down the monopoly of exclusively departmental concentrations should be done with considerable care. Courses brought together to create study in depth must not be a hodgepodge. On the other hand, there is nothing inherently coherent about a random selection of courses in one department. A requirement that all courses be taken in the department is no guarantee that the experience will truly be one in depth rather than in scattered exposure.

Study in depth, therefore, is not so much an additional component of the curriculum as it is recognition of the degree of complexity and sophistication with which the various components are interrelated and understood. Although the almost universal practice has been to organize the curriculum into disciplines and then have students "major" in one of them, what a valid discipline is and how many of them there are remains an open question. But depth, we are certain, does not arise merely from the existence of an extensive factual base. For our purposes a course of study has depth if it in fact offers a complex structure of knowledge. The comprehension of this structure —a decent understanding and control of it—is what we mean by study in depth.

Complex structures of knowledge may themselves differ substantially in character and still offer depth in our sense. The complexity of a field or discipline may derive predominantly from the intricacy of its materials—the fact that it brings together and comprehends different systems of knowledge, as in biochemistry and astronomy. It may derive predominantly from the continuous relevance of a substantial and cumulative history, as in literature and law; or from the crucial interplay between continuous observation on the one hand and a developing, articulated, theoretical base on the other, as in economics and physics.

In any case, study in depth requires multiple dimension; it cannot be reached merely by cumulative exposure to more and more of a specified subject matter. For instance, the study of literature is not requisitely deep if at the end the student has merely taken six or eight or ten courses in a literature department: there is no depth if the students have not brought into focus and appreciated in their interrelations a refined degree of literacy, an understanding of literature as cultural history, and a knowledge of the theory of how language and literature create meaning, and of the problems of reaching aesthetic judgments.

A course of study that offers depth will almost invariably exhibit certain features. It will have a central core of method and theory that serves as an introduction to the explanatory power of the discipline, provides a basis for subsequent work, and unites all students who join in the study in a shared understanding of its character and aims. It will force students to experience the range of topics that the discipline addresses and the variety of analytic tools that it uses. It will have a sequence that presumes advancing sophistication. It will provide a means — a project or a thesis — by which the student's final mastery of its complexity, however modest or provisional, may be demonstrated and validated. Study in depth should lead

students to some understanding of the discipline's characteristic questions and arguments, as well as the questions it cannot answer and the arguments it does not make. It should give students experience with the tools of the disciplines, acquaint them with their history and philosophical presuppositions, and provide them with a strong sense of their limits and power as instruments for understanding human society.

Prerequisites — courses that permit entry into other courses — suggest adherence to a belief in sequential learning, but too often prerequisites are political in origin and effect, subsidizing certain courses with students who neither want to be there nor should be there. But there certainly should be courses where well-considered prerequisites are educationally valid, where successful performance at a high level absolutely demands the knowledge or technique acquired in a previous course. As they advance, students should work increasingly with the primary materials of their concentration — texts, documents, artifacts, substances, works of art — and not with edited collections and laboratory codes. They should learn how to extract meaning from such materials, neither more nor less than the values and standards of the discipline allow. Every discipline, not just the sciences, should acquaint students with some of the "dead ends" of the field, notable experiments, theories, and intellectual and artistic undertakings that failed.

Concentration cannot and should not attempt to teach students everything they need to know — they have the rest of their lives for that, and even so they will fall short of any such unrealistic goal. Every cannonade from the "information explosion" does not require a spate of new courses and faculty appointments. The claims pressed for bringing the new and marvelous into the course of study in dramatic and expensive ways are false and distracting. If legitimate, they will make their way in time. The test is whether they are necessary to holding a college true to its mission of developing alert and inquiring students, ready to grow and serve themselves and their society as citizens.

The traditional academic disciplines offered for study in depth, if they have the requisite complexity, can be justified on that basis alone, as the ultimate intellectual exercise that gives students their first insight into the complexity of knowledge itself. But justified as they may be, they are not the only nor even necessarily the best ways to achieve depth. Many of these disciplines have an abstraction and a narrowness that do not recommend them to students who want this central effort in their college careers to lead with clearer relevance to their later lives, and who do not contemplate academic careers. For such students interdisciplinary studies and professional studies offer a powerful alternative, always providing that they offer the requisite complexity.

Interdisciplinary studies by their very nature tend to be complex: such subjects as area and period studies, women's studies, ethnic studies, by definition require the simultaneous comprehension of a variety of fields of knowledge. Where interdisciplinary studies are focused on major world problems—energy, population, de-velopment, conservation of natural resources—they offer an attractive bridge between intellectual discipline and career preparation. Real life, we need to remember, is interdisciplinary.

Education in a professional or vocational field may, if based on the skills and attitudes of our minimum curriculum and presented in a liberal spirit, also provide a strong, enriching form of study in depth. Contemporary technical and professional curricula, the lineal descendants of the new land-grant programs of a century ago, afford access to baccalaureate education for thousands of men and women otherwise unlikely to seek it. The danger to intellectual growth in such programs—just the opposite of the disarray in the central disciplines in the liberal arts colleges—is excessive structure and overprescription of training in currently fashionable technique, ephemeral information, and obsolescent technology. Students of professional fields, from chemical engineering to business to medical technology to music, also need the experiences of our required curriculum to inform their intensely focused concentration and to prepare them for responsible citizenship. They must learn critical analysis and the capacity to make decisions in uncertain settings with insufficient data; they must gain the ability to write and speak clearly, sometimes on life-or-death questions, to clients, employees, and professional communities; their future practice must be informed by constant awareness of the environmental and societal impact—human costs *vs.* political benefits, aesthetic enhancement or debasement—of the work to which they are committing their lives.

On such a base a sound professional education can be built.

Self-conscious examination of the claims and mode of the discipline, therefore, is equally as important in the professional fields as in the traditional ones. Engineering, business, allied health, and all the other professional undergraduate concentrations should be subjected to the same expectations as those in the arts and sciences. Just as students in professional programs should not be short-changed by being exempt from the minimum required curriculum, neither should professional study in depth be allowed to deliver experiences any less rewarding than those we consider integral to those in the arts and sciences. Courses in decision-making in a particular professional field should provide entry not simply to the nature of the profession, business or engineering, for example, but also to its theory, history, ethics, and style.

We believe that students intending to pursue careers in medicine should be qualified for admission to medical school upon completion of a program in undergraduate education such as is here projected. Our prescribed minimum curriculum is just as important for pre-medical students and science majors as for others. The science courses offered in the required curriculum should be as serviceable to prospective science majors and medical students as to others. It is time to wean faculties away from the excess that now characterizes the science requirements for pre-medical students. The medical schools must be encouraged to pay attention to the forceful critics who have risen from within their ranks. Doctors should have the benefit of the course of study we propose. There is no valid reason why physicians should be denied the educational advantages that will be enjoyed by lawyers, businessmen, artists, and all the others for whom the curriculum will be a liberating experience.

Study in depth, whether professional in focus or not, should not be overprescribed. Every requirement in it should be intellectually defensible. Nor should students be permitted to concentrate beyond necessity: excessive passion for a discipline should not be allowed to deny a student the opportunity to pursue a passing intellectual fancy. Study in depth should be just that and nothing more; it cannot be allowed to dominate the student's entire program, prescribing how the basic required curriculum is to be fulfilled, dictating core courses and other academic experiences. The discipline has done its job when it has illuminated the power of concentration and the strengths of its own approach.

Options for students to change direction should remain open as long as possible. Students may be trapped in the wrong concentration because they ignored the counsel of teachers and friends or misread their own hearts and minds. An educationally imaginative institution will make it possible for students to extricate themselves, unless it is structurally simply too late, from the wrong concentration. It is often possible to construct the beginnings of new study in depth from a student's completed courses, particularly in an environment where concentration and a discipline are not synonymous with a department.

Comprehensive examinations are an echo of the doctoral examinations of the graduate schools. Their appearance in undergraduate colleges had something to do with insinuating a semblance of coherence into a curriculum in disarray. They also allowed professors to hold students responsible for coverage—centuries, literary figures, artists, national histories, scientific experiments—that was not reflected in their course programs. Preparing for comprehensive examinations is probably not the best use of a student's time and may in fact be disruptive of other educational experiences coming to fruition toward the end of the senior year. Imaginative opportunities for experiencing achievement in study in depth can be created: it is possible to invent intellectual exercises that will allow students to demonstrate what they know and how well they have learned to synthesize without indulging in the frantic memorization and cult of coverage that characterized comprehensive examinations in their worst incarnation. It is possible to bring an education together without pulling a student apart.

Our report envisions the ideal but not the impossible. If we do not address the difference between appropriate courses for concentrators and non-concentrators, between lower division and upper division courses, it is largely because these are distinctions that support the conditions that we hope will be remedied. Just suppose that the focus of curriculum planners were the student instead of the department: would courses for concentrators and non-concentrators, lower and upper divisions, pre-professional and non-professional programs, be where colleges expended their energies? We doubt it.

Every course should be taught differently, as if it were the only course that defined the difference, for the student, between catching hold and falling off. To turn the baccalaureate experience around, to make it an opportunity for a student to establish a style and a certain kind of bravery in the presence of the uncertain and the unknown—that is the sort of event that colleges should be all about. The major as now offered does not do that. The study in depth that we advocate will do it, if administrators and professors can tear themselves away from unexamined assumptions and sentimental journeys to their own undergraduate years.

*T*he Problem of Accountability

One of the most remarkable and scandalous aspects of American higher education is the absence of traditions, practices, and methods of institutional and social accountability. The spirit of freedom and individual enterprise has supported non-accountability and underwritten a great deal of irresponsibility. In a society where survival and growth are often the only tests of virtue, colleges and universities have paid too little attention to the measures appropriate to an assessment of their performance. How can colleges and universities assure the American people and themselves that they are doing what they say they are doing? How does anyone know that the curriculum really "works"? There must be ways of demonstrating to state legislatures, students, and the public at large that the colleges know what they are doing (or do not know) and that they are doing it well (or poorly.) The colleges themselves must be held responsible for developing evaluations that the public can respect.

There are three main areas of assessment, three places where the effectiveness of an institution can be evaluated: students, programs, faculty. In all three, interrelated as they are and by necessity requiring concurrent attention, the professors are fundamentally responsible and therefore charged with designing and monitoring the mechanisms of assessment.

As for students, faculties must know the nature of the material with which they begin. What is the nature of the preparation, the degree of sophistication, the distance between performance and promise that each student brings to the campus? What is the range in the student body as a whole? As improved access to college increases the range and diversity of student capacities at entrance, the answers to these questions shape what teachers can do and should do. They cannot do their job well unless they are in possession of reliable information on who the students are.

By the same token, without some accurate sense of the progress with which students are establishing skills and mastering the capacities defined by the minimum required curriculum, a faculty can only guess at how well it is doing its job. Both the faculty and the students themselves need assurance of progress established by carefully conceived instruments, or the reassurance that, in the absence of progress, some changes will be made. Finally, by the time of graduation, both should possess some hard evidence of the cumulative difference that the curriculum has made in the capacity of students to function as effective human beings.

Courses, therefore, require the same degree of assessment to which students are subjected. Course syllabi, teaching methods, and examinations all enter into the way a course fails or succeeds. Teachers need to know which work best. Programs in colleges come and go, according to the whims of students and the interests of faculty, but seldom benefitting from the guidance of program evaluation and the assessment of the relationship between goals and results. As difficult as it may be to develop the most searching and appropriate methods of evaluation and assessment, an institution that lacks refined instruments of program evaluation and rigorous instruments of student assessment is contributing to the debasement of baccalaureate education.

As we have argued earlier, the process by which faculty are selected and faculty performance is evaluated and rewarded must be seriously re-examined in the light of a college's educational objectives. The criteria for hiring, promoting, and rewarding faculty must bear a close relationship to the institution's stated educational aims.

It is easy enough to announce what is desirable. It is just as easy to deplore the absence of reliable instruments for evaluating students, programs, and faculty, and for establishing expectations and practices of individual and corporate accountability. But the stark truth is that higher education is not yet in possession of generally useful means for the sophisticated assessment of the general worth of programs or of the integrated cumulative intellectual growth and capacities of students. There are many procedures available for assessing particular aspects of higher education, but the state of the art is either so primitive or tentative that we believe that there is need for a larger national program of support for the development of reliable and sensitive means of student and program evaluation.

We neither propose a national system of testing, inconsistent with our traditions and threatening to the kind of imaginative creativity that is a national resource, nor a continuation of the heedlessness that has spared our colleges and universities a strict accountability. Faculties can design their own procedures of assessment, and groups of related institutions can cooperate in creating valuable sources of comparison. Even without the results of the national program of development that we propose, much can be done to improve assessment through encouraging better means of serious communication between faculty and students, locating faculty responsibility in a faculty committee on assessment and giving it appropriate powers, and building time for responsible assessment into a professor's day. A joint trustee-faculty-student committee on assessment could oversee the legitimate interests and responsibilities of each group. Greater openness about the process of learning and teaching, a greater willingness to employ sound and responsible testing of students, and a continuous evaluation and interpretation of the results of educational programs need not await the sophisticated tools that are surely on the way.

*T*he Profession of College Teaching

While we have already drawn attention to the failure of graduate schools to prepare holders of the doctorate degree for careers in teaching, we want to consider the profession of college teaching more fully. The primary obligation of professionals is to know their professional business, its ethical responsibilities to clients and the profession itself, the skills essential to its performance, and the body of knowledge that must be mastered. The first obligation of a college teacher must, therefore, be to the profession of teaching.

Unfortunately for the development of a responsible profession of college teaching, the academic preparation of the typical faculty member is in a graduate program leading to the Ph.D. degree. The emphasis of the graduate school years is almost exclusively on the development of substantive knowledge and research skills. Any introduction to teaching comes only incidentally through service as a teaching assistant, with only occasional supervision by experienced senior faculty. During the long years of work toward the doctoral degree, the candidate is rarely, if ever, introduced to any of the ingredients that make up the art, the science, and the special responsibilities of teaching. Yet, the major career option for most holders of the Ph.D. degree is full-time teaching in a college or university.

The teaching assistantship is now a device for exploiting graduate students in order to relieve senior faculty from teaching undergraduates. The tradition in higher education is to award the degree and then turn the students loose to become teachers without training in teaching or, equally as ridiculous, to send the students off without degrees, with unfinished research and incomplete dissertations hanging over their heads while they wrestle with the responsibilities of learning how to teach. Only in higher education is it generally assumed that teachers need no preparation, no supervision, no introduction to teaching. Ironically, one of the reasons that universities have shirked their responsibilities to the schools and to their schools of education may be a refusal to take seriously the profession of teaching. If the professional preparation of doctors were as minimal as that of college teachers, the United States would have more funeral directors than lawyers.

Beginning teachers arrive at their college posts with memories of inspired teaching in their own undergraduate days, memories that are perhaps the surest guide they have to how to go

35

about being a college teacher. But they also have memories of teaching that was unimaginative, ineffective, and unworthy of a self-respecting profession. Candidates for the Ph.D. degree need more than memory as a guide and more than the typical unsupervised experience of the teaching assistant, thrown into a classroom of undergraduates as if it did not matter whether they knew what to do and how to do it. In fact, as an initiation rite, the teaching assistantship is almost invariably a disaster: it says to the initiate that teaching is so unimportant we are willing to let you do it. What *is* important, it says, is to demonstrate skills in the discipline, and the only way that matters is in research.

The Ph.D. candidate should be introduced in a systematic way to the profession of teaching. The qualifying process should include acquaintance with the literature on human learning and evaluation as well as apprentice teaching, subject to peer observation and the criticism of veteran teachers. The candidate should demonstrate competence in designing a syllabus and examinations, and selecting textbooks, readings, and laboratory materials. Not only must the candidate learn how to read tests critically but fairly and how to know the difference between a good paper subject and one that is either too grandiose or simply not worth doing. The grading of undergraduate papers and tests by teaching assistants must be carefully monitored and not allowed to degenerate into the objective testing and grading that neither tests the student critically and imaginatively nor requires much judgment on the part of the apprentice instructor.

The candidate should also receive instruction in how best to help students to speak and write clearly.

Certainly teaching assistants have much to learn from one another, but they can learn even more when candidates from various disciplines share their teaching experiences in a formal seminar directed by a veteran teacher. The same seminar could be a vehicle for leading apprentice teachers into an understanding of the ethical imperatives and responsibilities of teaching and of obligations to students, to institutions, and to the larger academic community.

The Ph.D. degree is now awarded only on the basis of an evaluation of a candidate's research skills. If teaching in American higher education is to become more effective and responsible, the awarding of the Ph.D. degree should also mean that the candidate has been evaluated as a teacher and not found wanting, and that the formal experience leading to the degree has included appropriate instruction in the responsibilities of the profession.

Programs of assistance and supervision of apprentice teachers, begun in the graduate schools, must continue in the colleges and universities where they gain employment. Institutions of higher education must demonstrate their commitment to teaching at the outset of every new appointment by offering a program which systematically helps the new recruits to improve their teaching styles and their intellectual reach. The first-year faculty member can profit from sharing a course with experienced colleagues and from visitations by senior colleagues, not necessarily limited to members of the instructor's department. Videotaping of an actual classroom session, done unobtrusively, has proved effective in encouraging self-evaluation. Teachers who arrive on campus with unfinished dissertations should be assisted by various institutional practices in hastening their completion: the burdens of beginning teaching, finishing a dissertation, and parenthood have visited much miserable teaching on the college classroom.

Unless the reward system in higher education measures teaching performance as well as research, all efforts to improve college teaching will be to no avail. Good teaching must contribute to the achievement of tenure, promotion, and salary advancement. Colleagues have an easier time evaluating research, often calling on external disciplinary evaluators, excusing poor teaching if the research is notable, downgrading good teaching if the research is negligible. If departments are to evaluate fairly and take seriously their responsibility to teaching, they must provide themselves as well with all kinds of evidence that illuminate the teaching contribution: reports by senior colleagues, videotapes, critical analyses of syllabi and tests, grading practices, student evaluation, and interviews with students selected by both the instructor and the department. Dependence on any one of these possible kinds of evidence is of course unfair to the instructor and to the process of evaluation. Research and study are an aspect of a teacher's intellectual quality and liveliness and should also be measured in any assessment of a teacher's effectiveness and capacity for growth. The best teachers have found ways to use research as a con-

tinuing exercise in intellectual growth and as a means of enriching their teaching. Ideal teachers, of course, never allow themselves to accept the false dichotomy between teaching and research and study: they embrace both and are dominated by neither.

Among encouraging signs that teaching can be taken seriously are the use of the "contract" for professional development by which faculty members reach agreement with their institutions concerning goals over a specified period of years, external reviews of programs and syllabi by expert colleagues, and recognition through presentation in professional journals and organizations. Particularly welcome is the involvement of the established professional societies, such as the American Philosophical Association, the Modern Language Association, and the American Chemical Society in focusing attention on successful teaching experiences, providing bibliographical and other teaching resources, and recognizing the relationship between teaching and the health of the disciplines.

There are special obligations that flow from being a college teacher. Some of them are often ignored, some are given lip service, but all must be adhered to if the profession of college teaching is to develop the self-regulation, set of guiding ethics, shared identity, and sense of community that denote a true profession. Thus far in the history of American higher education we have had professional sociologists, professional geologists, and professional practitioners of all the other disciplines, but the profession of college teaching to which they all belong has been slow to assert the set of skills and obligations necessary to its practice.

Among those obligations, we believe, is the responsibility of faculty to teach undergraduates a significant portion of the year. We are talking about all —not some—faculty, senior no less than junior, research university faculties no less than college faculties. All college and university teachers must be committed, beyond their disciplines and departments, to the educational ideals of the institution. Effective and responsible teaching not only enhances the subject under study but illuminates the general objectives of the curriculum and fulfills the obligations of the institution to humanistic values and concerns. Students also have every reason to expect that their teachers will provide them with ample office hours—hours that they will honor, that the tests and papers that are a part of the learning process will be fairly graded, promptly returned, and provided with helpful comment by the instructor.

The corporate responsibility of the faculty for the curriculum as a whole extends also to responsibility for forceful defense of academic freedom. In their special responsibilities to students, college and university teachers are required, however, not to use the classroom as a platform for propagandizing. Professional ethics demand that they be balanced and that they be fair. Instruction is an instrument of inquiry, not indoctrination. Inquiry requires freedom, indoctrination stifles it. Professors, by virtue of their responsibilities and privileges in learned positions of great public trust, must place the interests, welfare, and legitimate rights of students above all other considerations; that is what constitutes a professional relationship.

We look forward to the development of a self-conscious profession of college teaching, replete with all the appurtenances appropriate to a proud and honored profession: its own professional organization, journals, and arbiters of professional matters. It is instructive that the disciplines have banded together as the American Council of Learned Societies and the American Association for the Advancement of Science, but they have banded together not as teachers but as intellectuals and guardians of their disciplines. Nor have the American Association of University Professors nor the American Federation of Teachers become instruments for defining and nurturing the idea of college and university teaching as a profession. The disciplines themselves offer possible models in the teaching-based organizations of college and secondary faculties—The American Association of Teachers of French, the American Association of Physics Teachers, the National Council of Teachers of English—that have worked for classroom improvement. The groundwork has been done. A profession can be built.

The public at large and the academic community itself are uneasy with the evidence of the decline and devaluation of the bachelor's degree in the recent past. To restore integrity to the bachelor's degree there must be a renewal of the faculty's corporate responsibility for the curriculum. We propose a minimum required curriculum of nine basic intellectual, aesthetic, and philosophic experiences as a design for diverting the course of study from chaos. It points students in the direction of growth, skills, mastery, the insights and style necessary to responsible citizenship and the enjoyment of life in the decades ahead. To implement that process we encourage a reassessment of the profession of college teaching in the United States and the development and greater use of reliable instruments of evaluation.

The widespread critical assault on all aspects of American education carries a special message to the colleges and universities. They will have to do a better job in order to regain lost support and in order to fulfill their responsibilities to themselves, their students, and the society that depends on them. To that end we offer this report.

Appendix

General Reports Relating to Secondary and Collegiate Education

Academic Preparation for College: What Students Need to Know and Be Able to Do. New York: The College Board/Educational Equality Project, May 1983.

This proposed agenda for high schools to pursue presents a comprehensive description of what college entrants need to learn in six basic academic subjects (English, the arts, mathematics, science, social studies, foreign language) that provide the knowledge and skills for successful college-level study. Similarly it describes those general skills and abilities necessary for effective work in all subjects in six basic academic competencies (reading, writing, speaking and listening, mathematics, reasoning, and studying). There is an additional statement on the emerging need for computer competency. The booklet does not discuss everything (such as social and coping skills) necessary for effective work in college; its topic is limited to academic preparation.

Action for Excellence. Denver: Task Force on Education For Economic Growth/Education Commission of the States, June 1983.

This report emphasizes that the new age of technology and global competition is changing our concept of basic skills which its sees as "those skills necessary for a person's economic competence." It notes the immediate problem of low enrollment in math and science courses and then outlines an "action plan" to encourage states to improve public education K-12. Some of the recommendations include: the creation of partnerships between business, labor, and the professions with the schools; the improvement of methods for recruiting, training, and paying teachers; the establishment of more demanding requirements concerning discipline, homework, grades, and other essentials; an increase in the duration of academic learning; and a tightening of the procedures used to certify, reward, retain, and dismiss teachers.

Curriculum: A History of the American Undergraduate Course of Study since 1636, by Frederick Rudolph. San Francisco: Jossey-Bass, 1979.

This book provides a comprehensive survey of the evolution of curriculum planning in American colleges and universities. Beginning with Harvard and continuing through other colonial colleges, the land-grant movement, and more recent developments, some of the more basic values and issues underlying specific curriculum orientations are presented. The author points out that the curriculum has been subject to changes, revisions, and updating through the years. These changes have not always kept pace with student needs, nor have they been very systematic or organized. He suggests that there is probably no such thing as the "one curriculum," since it always reflects a particular institutional philosophy.

Educating Americans for the 21st Century. Washington, D.C.: National Science Board Commission on Precollege Education in Mathematics, Science and Technology/National Science Foundation, September 1983.

This is a plan of action for improving elementary and secondary education in these fields so that American students can be "the best in the world by 1995." This will require changes in both what is learned and how it is taught including: greater time being devoted to the study of mathematics, science and technology; an improvement in the quality of teaching and an increase in the numbers of committed teachers; the inclusion of technology in mathematics, science, and other subjects; and the review and improvement of course substance including both texts and appropriate methodology. There are approximately 50 recommendations grouped by: leadership; focus on all students; quality teaching and earlier and increased exposure; models for change; solutions to the teaching dilemma; improving what is taught and learned; new information technologies; informal education; and finance. The report discusses minimum requirements for primary and secondary teachers, and suggests curriculum goals for all students at the primary and secondary levels.

High School: A Report on Secondary Education in America, by Ernest L. Boyer. [Princeton, N.J.: The Carnegie Foundation for the Advancement of Teaching.] New York: Harper & Row, 1983.

Much of this study is based on observations of life and work at 15 schools selected for inclusion in the Carnegie project. Boyer describes classes, teachers, students, and principals at these schools and then presents an "Agenda for Action" which is centered on his explicit essential tool—literacy. High School stresses that "teaching students to write clearly and effectively should be a central objective of the school" especially since "thought and language are inextricably connected." In addition the author asserts that technological literacy is more urgent than computer literacy and calls for all students to study "man's use of tools, how science and technology have been joined, and the ethical and social issues technology has raised." Besides specific recommendations for the core curriculum, there are a total of 29 recommendations about teachers and teaching.

Involvement in Learning: Realizing the Potential of American Higher Education. Washington, D.C.: Study Group on the Conditions of Excellence in American Higher Education, National Institute of Education/U.S. Department of Education, October, 1984.

The Study Group asserts that despite significant success in adapting to growth and change in recent years, all is not well in American higher education. Among the reasons cited are: only half of those who enter college for a bachelor's degree eventually receive it; colleges and universities have become excessively vocational in their orientation; curricula have become fragmented, and the ideal of the integration of knowledge has been diminished; colleges offer fewer opportunities for students to become involved with academic life; and few colleges examine the learning and growth of the students they graduate. The Report's 27 recommendations include: the incorporation by faculty of active modes of teaching that require students to take greater responsibility for their learning; the creation of learning communities, organized around specific intellectual themes or tasks; two full years of liberal education for all bachelor's degree recipients; regular student evaluations of the learning environment; and proficiency assessments in liberal arts and the student's major to supplement the credit system.

Making the Grade. New York: Task Force on Federal Elementary and Secondary Education Policy/Twentieth Century Fund, 1983.

The major recommendations of this report include: 1) the identification by the federal government that the most important objective of elementary and secondary education is the development of literacy in the English language; 2) the establishment of a federally funded Master Teachers Program to reward teaching excellence and to open the way for reconsideration of merit-based personnel systems that will keep the master teachers in the classroom; and 3) federal funds now going for bilingual education should be used to teach non-English-speaking children how to speak, read, and write English. Further, the report holds that "schools across the nation must at a minimum provide the same core components to all students. . .the basic skills of reading, writing and calculating; technical capability in computers; training in science and foreign languages; and knowledge of civics. . . ."

Missions of the College Curriculum. (A Commentary of the Carnegie Foundation for the Advancement of Teaching.) San Francisco: Jossey-Bass, 1977.

A comprehensive treatment of the curriculum that discusses factors influencing the curriculum, relationship of education to work and to society, and evaluation of the curriculum's effectiveness. Treats the essential aspects of the curriculum including the core, major, electives, and general education. Suggests directions for updating and reforming current courses of study.

A Nation at Risk: The Imperative for Education Reform. Washington, D.C.:
National Commission on Excellence in Education/U.S. Department of
Education, April 1983.

The primary imperative for reform is that "more and more young people
emerge from high school ready neither for college nor for work. . .[they
are] effectively disenfranchised." Five major recommendations follow:
1) the strengthening of state and local high school graduation requirements in English, mathematics, science, social studies, and computer
science; 2) the adoption by schools, colleges, and universities of more
rigorous and measurable standards and the raising of admission requirements by four-year colleges and universities; 3) the use of more time for
learning with an increase in homework assignments and a lengthening of
the school day and school year; 4) the improvement of teacher preparation and the demonstration of both an aptitude for teaching and competence in an academic discipline accompanied by increased salaries and
recognition of master teachers; and 5) the support of citizens in providing
fiscal support and stability required to bring about these reforms and
the responsibilities of educators and elected officials to provide the leadership necessary to achieve these goals.

A Place Called School: Prospects for the Future, by John I. Goodlad. New
York: McGraw-Hill, 1983.

Based on the author's eight-year long "Study of Schooling" which exam-
ined the perceptions of teachers, students and parents in 38 schools in
seven sections of the country. Goodlad describes their perceptions of
their schools' goals, leadership, curricula, instruction, counseling, etc.
and then discusses them in the light of his own. The goals of schooling
are rarely spelled out and Goodlad cites the states as the authority pri-
marily responsible for this. Further he concludes that his sample schools
do *not* appear to be developing those qualities commonly listed under
intellectual development. The author sees the passive acceptance of the
educational status quo as the greatest single deterent to change and
offers suggestions for overcoming this in the final two chapters,
"Improving the Schools We Have" and "Beyond the Schools We Have."

Three Thousand Futures: The Next Twenty Years For Higher Education.
Final Report of the Carnegie Council on Policy Studies. San Francisco:
Jossey-Bass, 1980.

The last in the series of reports issued by the Carnegie Council on Policy
Studies in Higher Education, this book considers American higher education in light of population shifts, budgetary restrictions, and an ever-
changing student body. Because these factors affect different institutions
differently, it is imperative for the leadership of each institution to make
its own projections. Part one provides a general analysis of enrollment
declines, shifting patterns of funding, and changes in the labor market

for college graduates. Part two consists of resource documents used by the Council for formulating its conclusions and recommendations. In sum, this report outlines actions administrators should take to assess institutional needs and to prepare for the future.

Forthcoming

College: A Report on Undergraduate Education in America, by Ernest L. Boyer. This study of the state of undergraduate education is to be published by Harper and Row in 1986.

Reports Relating to Disciplinary Areas

Beyond Growth: The Next Stage in Language and Area Studies, by Richard D. Lambert et al. Washington, D.C.: Association of American Universities, April 1984.

This report results from a year-long study of the current status of language and area studies in the U.S., a survey conducted for the Department of Defense under an NEH grant. Though the special concerns of these agencies are specifically addressed, the report is written "from the broader perspective of the national interests." The report concentrates on the present capacities of the nation's universities for advanced training and research in foreign language and area studies as a basis for the nation's security and foreign policy. "More generally, [it] documents the overall condition of university programs in language and area studies and recommends strategies for strengthening them." The recommendations deal with language and area competency, research, campus centers, national organizations, library and information services, and funding.

Physicians for the Twenty-First Century. Report of the Panel on the General Professional Education of the Physician and College Preparation for Medicine. Washington, D.C.: Association of American Medical Colleges, 1984.

The GPEP project assessed current approaches in medical education and college preparation for medicine; its primary concern was with the educational experience that precedes and prepares the physician for specialized education. Its major premise is that "all physicians, regardless of specialty, require a common foundation of knowledge, skills, values, and attitudes." There are five major conclusions with accompanying recommendations, and conclusion #2 focuses on baccalaureate education. In it the Panel notes that "college faculties by not defining and requiring both depth and breadth for the education of their students, reinforce their student's tendencies toward narrow, premature specialization." The recommendations stress broad, rigorous education in the social sciences and humanities, as well as the sciences, and urge modifications in medical schools' admission requirements and selection criteria.

45

To Reclaim a Legacy: A Report on the Humanities in Higher Education, by William J. Bennett. Washington, D.C.: National Endowment for the Humanities, November 1984.

The main theme of this report is that colleges and universities are failing to give students "an adequate education in the culture and civilization of which they are members." Evidence to support this claim includes facts such as: a student can obtain a bachelor's degree from 75 percent of all American colleges and universities without having studied European history, 72 percent without having studied American literature or history; and fewer than half of all colleges and universities require foreign language study for the bachelor's degree. The report recommends that all students encounter a "core of common studies" to include a chronological understanding of the development of Western civilization; careful reading of several masterworks of English, American, and European literature; demonstrable proficiency in a foreign language, modern or classical; and familiarity with at least one non-western culture or civilization. Colleges are urged to reward faculty for teaching as well as for research and to place the humanities at the center of instruction. The humanities, properly taught, "bring together the perennial questions of human life with the greatest works of history, literature, philosophy and art."

Science for Non-Specialists: The College Years. Report of the National Research Council's Committee on a Study of the Federal Role in College Science Education of Non-Specialists. Washington, D.C.: National Academy Press, 1982.

The Committee had a three-fold task as its charge: 1) to determine how science is being presented to undergraduate students who are not studying to become scientists; 2) to recommend improvements that may be needed in what is perceived to be a neglected branch of undergraduate education; and 3) to determine if there is a role for the federal government in assisting colleges and universities to meet their responsibilities to provide their students with an appropriate science education. The report stresses that college science education "should enable non-specialists to gain the scientific and technical knowledge needed to fulfill civic responsibilities in society" and in leadership roles in their own fields. It urges the federal government, specifically through the National Science Foundation, to establish a vigorous program for these purposes.

Wingspread Reports, Washington, D.C.: Association of American Colleges:

Toward Education with a Global Perspective. A Report of The National Assembly on Foreign Language and International Studies, 1980.

Widening the Circle: The Humanities in American Life. A Report of the Wingspread Conference on the Humanities in Higher Education, 1981.

Liberal Education and the New Scholarship on Women: Issues and Constraints in Institutional Change. A Report of the Wingspread Conference, 1981.

Science and Technology Education for Civic and Professional Life: The Undergraduate Years. A Report of the Wingspread Conference, 1982.